Home

First presented by The English Stage Company on June 17th, 1970, at the Royal Court Theatre with the following cast of characters:

Harry	John Gielgud
Jack	Ralph Richardson
Alfred	Warren Clarke
Marjorie	Dandy Nichols
Kathleen	Mona Washbourne

The play directed by Lindsay Anderson
Setting by Jocelyn Herbert

The action passes on the terrace of a house

ACT I Scene 1	Morning
Scene 2	A short time later
ACT II	Afternoon

Time: the present

ACT I

Scene 1

There is a white flag-pole RC, *and upstage a low terrace with a single step down,* C; *and a balustrade* L. *A round metalwork table is set slightly off-centre* L, *with a metalwork chair on either side.*

When the CURTAIN *rises, the stage is empty. After a moment Harry comes on up* R. *He wears a casual suit, perhaps tweed, with a suitable hat which, after glancing pleasurably around, he takes off, coming down* C. *He puts his hat on the table, along with a pair of well-used leather gloves and a folded newspaper. He sits on the chair* L *of the table, presses his shoulders back, eases his neck, etc., making himself comfortable. He settles down. He glances at his watch shakes it, makes sure it's going, winds it slowly, looking round. He stretches his neck again, leans down, wafts cotton from his turn-ups, examines his shoes without stooping. He clears his throat, clasps his hands in his lap, gazes out, abstracted, his head nodding slightly, half-smiling.*

Jack Harry!

Jack has entered up L. *He is dressed in similar fashion, but with a slightly more dandyish flavour: handkerchief hanging from top pocket, a rakish trilby: he carries, too, a simple though rather elegant cane.*

Harry Jack.
Jack Been here long?
Harry No. No.
Jack You mind?
Harry Not at all.
Jack (*sitting down*) Nice to see the sun again. (*He stretches, shows great relief at being off his feet, etc*)
Harry Very.
Jack Been laid up for a few days.
Harry Oh dear.
Jack Chill. In bed.

Harry Oh, dear. Still . . . appreciate the comforts.
Jack What? You're right. Still—nice to be out.
Harry 'Tis.
Jack Mind?
Harry All yours.

Jack picks up the paper and gazes at it without unfolding it

Jack Damn bad news.
Harry Yes.
Jack Not surprising.
Harry Gets worse before it gets better.
Jack S'right. Still—not to grumble.
Harry No. No.
Jack Put on a bold front. (*He turns the paper over*)
Harry That's right.
Jack (*indicating the paper*) Pretty.
Harry Very.
Jack By Jove . . . (*He reads intently for a moment*) Oh, well.
Harry That the one? (*He glances over*)
Jack Yes. Tch, tch, tch!
Harry Ah, well. (*He shakes his head*)
Jack Yes. Still . . .
Harry Clouds—watch their different shapes.
Jack Yes? (*He looks up at the sky, at which Harry is gaping*)
Harry See how they drift over?
Jack By Jove.
Harry First sight—nothing. Then—just watch the edges . . . See.
Jack Amazing.
Harry Never notice when you're just walking.
Jack No. Still—best time of the year.
Harry What?
Jack Always think this the best time.
Harry Oh, yes.
Jack Not too hot. Not too cold.
Harry (*pointing at the paper*) Seen that?
Jack (*reading*) By Jove! (*He reads again briefly*) Well—you get some surprises. Hello (*He reads further down, turning the edge of the paper over*) Good God.
Harry What I felt.
Jack The human mind. (*He shakes his head*)
Harry Oh dear, yes.
Jack One of these days . . .
Harry Ah, yes.
Jack Then where will they be?
Harry Oh, yes.
Jack Never give it a thought.
Harry No. Never.
Jack (*reading again*) By Jove . . . (*He shakes his head*)

Harry leans over and removes something casually from Jack's sleeve

Harry Cotton.
Jack Oh. Picked it up . . . (*He glances round at the other sleeve, then down at his trousers*)
Harry See you've come prepared.
Jack What? . . . Oh.

Harry indicates Jack's coat pocket. Jack takes out a folded plastic mac, no larger, folded, than his hand

  Best to make sure.
Harry Took a risk. Myself.
Jack Oh, yes. . . . What's life worth . . .
Harry Oh, yes.
Jack I say. That was a shock.
Harry Yesterday . . . ?
Jack Bolt from the blue, and no mistake.
Harry I'd been half-prepared—even then.
Jack Still: a shock.
Harry Absolutely.
Jack My wife—you've met?—was that last week?
Harry Ah, yes . . .
Jack Well. A very delicate woman.
Harry Still. Very sturdy.
Jack Oh, well. Physically, nothing to complain of.
Harry Oh, no.
Jack Temperament, however . . . inclined to the sensitive side.
Harry Really.
Jack Two years ago . . . (*He glances off stage*) By Jove. Isn't that Saxton?
Harry Believe it is.
Jack He's a sharp dresser, and no mistake.
Harry Very.
Jack They tell me . . . Well, I never.
Harry Didn't see that, did he? (*They laugh, looking off*) Eyes in the back of your head these days.
Jack You have. That's right.
Harry Won't do that again in a hurry. What? (*He laughs*)
Jack I had an uncle once who bred horses.
Harry Really.
Jack Used to go down there when I was a boy.
Harry The country.
Jack Nothing like it. What? Fresh air.
Harry Clouds. (*He gestures up*)
Jack I'd say so.
Harry *My* wife was coming up this morning.
Jack Really?
Harry Slight headache. Thought might be better . . .
Jack Indoors. Well. Best make sure.

Harry When I was in the army . . .

Jack Really? What regiment?

Harry Fusiliers.

Jack Really? How extraordinary.

Harry You?

Jack No. No. A cousin.

Harry Well . . .

Jack Different time, of course.

Harry Ah.

Jack Used to bring his rifle . . . No. That was Arthur. Got them muddled. (*He laughs*)

Harry Still.

Jack Never leaves you.

Harry No. No.

Jack In good stead.

Harry Oh, yes.

Jack All your life.

Harry Oh, yes.

Jack I was—for a very short while—in the Royal Air Force.

Harry Really?

Jack Nothing to boast about.

Harry Oh, now. Flying?

Jack On the ground.

Harry (*after a pause*) Crysanthemums is my wife's hobby.

Jack Really.

Harry Thirty-seven species round the house.

Jack Beautiful flower.

Harry Do you know there are over a hundred?

Jack Really?

Harry Different species.

Jack Suppose you can mix them up.

Harry Oh. Very.

Jack He's coming back . . .

Harry looks enquiringly

Swanson.

Harry Saxton.

Jack Saxton! Always did get those two mixed up. Two boys at school: one called Saxton, the other Swanson. The curious thing is, they both looked alike.

Harry Really?

Jack Both had a curious skin disease. Here. Just at the side of the nose.

Harry Eczema.

Jack Really?

Harry Could have been.

Jack Never thought of that. . . . (*He pauses*) When I was young I had an ambition to be a priest, you know.

Harry Really?

Jack Thought about it a great deal.

Harry Ah, yes. A great decision.

Jack Oh, yes.

Harry Catholic or Anglican?

Jack Well, I could never quite make up my mind.

Harry Both got a great deal to offer.

Jack Great deal? My word.

Harry Advantages one way. And then—in another.

Jack Oh, yes.

Harry One of my first ambitions . . .

Jack Yes.

Harry Oh, now. You'll laugh.

Jack No. No—No. Really.

Harry Well—I would have liked to have been a dancer.

Jack Dancer—Tap or "balley"?

Harry Oh, well. Probably a bit of both.

Jack A fine thing. Grace.

Harry Ah, yes.

Jack Physical momentum.

Harry Yes.

Jack Swanson might have appreciated that!

Harry Saxton.

Jack Saxton! By Jove—At school we had a boy called Ramsbottom.

Harry Really.

Jack Now, I wouldn't have envied that boy's life.

Harry No.

Jack The euphemisms to which a name—well. One doesn't have to think very far.

Harry No.

Jack A name can be a great embarrassment in life.

Harry It can. We had—let me think—a boy called Fish.

Jack Fish!

Harry And another called Parsons!

Jack Parsons!

Harry Nicknamed "Nosey".

Jack By Jove! (*He laughs and rises*) Some of these nicknames are very clever.

Harry Yes.

Jack (*moving away* R) I remember when I was young, I had a very tall friend—extremely tall as a matter of fact. He was called "Lolly".

Harry Lolly!

Jack It fitted him very well. He . . . (*there is an abstracted pause*) Yes. Had very large teeth as well.

Harry The past. It conjures up some images.

Jack Oh, it does. It does. You're right.

Harry You wonder how there was ever time for it all.

Jack Time—Oh—don't mention it.

Harry A fine cane.

Jack What? Oh, that.

Harry Father had a cane. Walked for miles.

Jack A habit that's fast dying out.

Harry Oh, yes.

Jack Knew a man, related to a friend on my father's side, who used to walk twenty miles a day.

Harry Twenty!

Jack Each morning.

Harry That really shows some spirit.

Jack If you keep up a steady pace, you can manage four miles in the hour.

Harry Goodness.

Jack Five hours. Set off at eight each morning. Back for lunch at one.

Harry Must have had a great appetite.

Jack Absolutely. Ate like a horse.

Harry Stand him in good stead later on.

Jack Yes. Killed, you know. In the war.

Harry Oh, dear.

Jack Funny thing to work out.

Harry Oh, yes.

There is a pause

Jack (*sitting*) You do much fighting?

Harry What?

Jack Army.

Harry Oh, well. Then—modest amount.

Jack Nasty business.

Harry Doesn't bear thinking about.

Jack Two relatives of mine killed in the war.

Harry Oh, dear.

Jack You have to give thanks, I must say.

Harry Oh, yes.

Jack Mother's father—a military man.

Harry Yes.

Jack All his life.

Harry He must have seen some sights.

Jack Oh, yes.

Harry Must have all had meaning then.

Jack Oh, yes. Africa. India. He's buried, as a matter of fact, in Hong Kong.

Harry Really?

Jack So they tell me. Never been there myself.

Harry No.

Jack Hot climates, I think, can be the very devil if you haven't the temperament.

Harry Huh! You don't have to tell me.

Jack Been there?

Harry No, no. Just what one reads.

Jack Dysentery.

Harry Beriberi.

Jack Yellow fever.

Harry Oh, dear.

Jack To say nothing of the other contingencies.

Harry Oh, yes.

Jack At times one's glad simply to live on an island.

Harry Yes.

Jack Strange that.

Harry Yes.

Jack Without the sea—all around—civilization would never have been the same.

Harry No.

Jack The ideals of life, liberty, freedom, could never have been the same—democracy—well, if we'd been living on the continent, for example.

Harry Absolutely.

Jack Are those your gloves?

Harry Yes.

Jack I've got a pair like that at home.

Harry Yes.

Jack Very nearly. The seam goes the other way I think. (*He picks up a glove and looks at it*) Yes. It does.

Harry A present.

Jack Oh, yes?

Harry My wife. At Christmas.

Jack Season of good cheer.

Harry Less and less, of course, these days.

Jack Oh, my dear man. The whole thing has been ruined. The moment money intrudes—all feeling goes straight out of the window.

Harry Oh, yes.

Jack I had an aunt once who owned a little shop.

Harry Really?

Jack Made almost her entire income during the few weeks before Christmas.

Harry Really.

Jack Never seemed to occur to her there was any ethical consideration.

Harry Oh, dear.

Jack Ah, well.

Harry Still . . .

Jack Apart from that, she was a very wonderful person.

Harry It's very hard to judge.

Jack It is.

Harry I have a car for instance.

Jack Yes?

Harry One day, in December, I happened to knock a pedestrian over in the street.

Jack Oh, dear.

Harry It was extremely crowded.

Jack You don't have to tell me. I've seen them.

Harry Happened to see something they wanted the other side. Dashed across. Before you know where you are . . .

Jack Not serious, I hope?

Harry No. No. No. Fractured arm.

Jack From that, you know, they might learn a certain lesson.

Harry Oh, yes.

Jack Experience is a stern master.

Harry Ah, yes. But then . . .

Jack Perhaps the only one.

Harry It is.

Jack I had a cousin, on my mother's side, who once fell off a cliff.

Harry Really.

Jack Quite a considerable height.

Harry Ah, yes.

Jack Fell into the sea, fortunately. Dazed. Apart from that, quite quickly recovered.

Harry Very fortunate.

Jack Did it for a dare. Only twelve years old at the time.

Harry I remember I fell off a cliff, one time.

Jack Oh, dear.

Harry Not very high. And there was someone there to catch me. (*He laughs*)

Jack They can be very exciting places.

Harry Oh, very.

Jack I remember I once owned a little boat.

Harry Really.

Jack For fishing. Nothing very grand.

Harry A fishing man.

Jack Not really. More an occasional pursuit.

Harry I've always been curious about that.

Jack Yes?

Harry "A solitary figure crouched upon a bank."

Jack Never stirring.

Harry No. No.

Jack Can be very tedious, I know.

Harry Still. A boat is more interesting.

Jack Oh, yes. A sort of tradition, really.

Harry In the family.

Jack No. No. More in the—island, you know.

Harry Ah, yes.

Jack Drake.

Harry Yes!

Jack Nelson.

Harry Beatty.

Jack Sir Walter Raleigh.

Harry There was a very fine man—poet.

Jack Lost his head, you know.

Harry It's surprising the amount of dust that collects in so short a space of time. (*He runs his hand lightly over the table*)

Jack It is. (*He looks round*) Spot like this, perhaps, attracts it.

Harry Yes . . . (*A pause*) You never became a priest, then?

Jack No . . . No.

Harry Splendid to have a vocation.

Jack 'Tis . . . Something you believe in.

Harry Oh, yes.

Jack I could never resolve certain difficulties myself.

Harry Yes?

Jack The how's and the wherefore's I could understand. How we came to be, and His presence lurking everywhere, you know, but as to the "why" —I could never understand. Seemed a terrible waste of time to me.

Harry Oh, yes.

Jack Thought it better to leave it to those who didn't mind.

Harry Ah, yes.

Jack The same was true, I suppose, about dancing.

Harry Oh, yes. I remember turning up for instance, to my first class, only to discover that all the rest of them were girls.

Jack Really?

Harry Well—there are men dancers, I know. Still . . . took up football after that.

Jack To professional standard, I imagine.

Harry Oh, no. Just the odd kick around. Joined a team that played in the park on Sunday mornings.

Jack The athletic life has many attractions.

Harry It has. It has.

There is a pause

Jack How long you been here, then?

Harry Oh, a couple of—er.

Jack Strange—meeting the other day.

Harry Yes.

Jack Said to myself as I went back, "What a chance encounter."

Harry Yes.

Jack So rare, these days, to meet someone to whom one can actually talk.

Harry I know what you mean.

Jack One works. One looks around. One meets people. But very little communication actually takes place.

Harry Very.

Jack None at all in most cases! (*He laughs*)

Harry Oh, absolutely.

Jack The agonies and frustrations. I can assure you. In the end one gives up in absolute despair.

Harry Oh, yes. (*He laughs, rising and looking off*)

Jack (*looking off*) Isn't that Parker?

Harry No. N-no. Believe his name is Fielding.

Jack Could have sworn it was Parker.

Harry No. Don't think so—Parker walks with a limp. Very slight.

Jack That's Marshall.

Harry Really. Then I've got Parker mixed up again. (*He laughs*)

Jack Did you see the one who came in yesterday?

Harry Hendricks.

Jack Is that his name?

Harry I believe that's what I heard.

Jack He looked a very suspicious-looking character, I thought. And his wife . . .

Harry I would have thought his girl-friend.

Jack Really? Oh well, that makes far more sense—I mean, I have great faith in the institution of marriage as such.

Harry Oh, yes.

Jack But one thing I've always noticed. When you find a married couple who display their affection in public, then that's an infallible sign that their marriage is breaking up.

Harry Really? (*He crosses* R)

Jack It's a very curious thing. I'm sure there must be some psychological explanation for it.

Harry Insecurity. (*He looks off* R)

Jack Yes, I suppose so.

Harry Quite frequently one can judge people entirely by their behaviour.

Jack You can. I believe you're right.

Harry Take my father, for instance.

Jack Oh, yes.

Harry Extraordinary man by any standards. And yet, throughout his life, he could never put out a light.

Jack Really.

Harry Superstition. If he had to turn off a switch, he'd ask someone else to do it. (*Crossing back* L)

Jack How extraordinary.

Harry Quite casually. One never noticed. Over the years one got quite used to it of course. As a man he was extremely polite.

Jack Ah, yes.

Harry (*sitting*) Mother, now. She was quite the reverse.

Jack Oh, yes.

Harry Great appetite for life.

Jack Really?

Harry Three.

Jack Three?

Harry Children.

Jack Oh, really?

Harry Youngest.

Jack You were?

Harry Oh, yes.

Jack One of seven.

Harry Seven!

Jack Large families in those days.

Harry Oh, yes.

Jack Family life.

Harry Oh, yes.

Jack Society, well, without it, wouldn't be what it is today.

Harry Oh, no.
Jack Still.
Harry Oh, yes.
Jack We have a very wonderful example.
Harry Oh. My word.
Jack At times, I don't know where some of us would be without it.
Harry No. Not at all.
Jack A friend of mine—actually, more of an acquaintance, really—was introduced to George the Sixth at Waterloo.
Harry Waterloo?

There is a pause

Jack The station.
Harry By Jove.
Jack He was an assistant to the station-master at the time, in a lowly capacity, of course. His Majesty was taking a week-end trip into the country.
Harry Probably to Windsor.
Jack (*after a pause*) Can you get to Windsor from Waterloo?
Harry I'm . . . No. I'm not sure.
Jack Sandringham, of course, is in the country.
Harry The other way.
Jack The other way.
Harry Balmoral in the Highlands.
Jack I had an aunt once who, for a short while, lived near Gloucester.
Harry That's a remarkable stretch of the country.
Jack Vale of Evesham.
Harry Vale of Evesham.
Jack Local legend has it that Adam and Eve originated there.
Harry Really?
Jack Has very wide currency, I believe, in the district. For instance. You may have read that portion in the Bible . . .
Harry I have.
Jack The profusion of vegetation, for example, would indicate that it couldn't, for instance, be anywhere in the Middle East.
Harry No. No.
Jack On the other hand, the profusion of animals—snakes, for example— would indicate that it might easily be a more tropical environment, as opposed that is to one which is merely temperate.
Harry Yes—I see.
Jack Then again, there is ample evidence to suggest that during the period in question the equatorial conditions prevailed in the very region in which we are now sitting.
Harry Really? (*Looking round*)
Jack Discoveries have been made that would indicate that lions and tigers, elephants, wolves, rhinoceros, and so forth, actually inhabited these parts.
Harry My word.

Jack In those circumstances, it wouldn't be unreasonable to suppose that the Vale of Evesham was such a place itself. The very cradle, as it were, of . . .

There is a pause

Harry Close to where your aunt lived.
Jack That's right.
Harry (*looking at Jack's cane*) Mind if I have a look?
Jack No, not at all.

Harry takes the cane

Harry One seldom sees canes of this quality these days.
Jack No. No. That's right.
Harry I believe they've gone out of fashion.
Jack They have.
Harry Like beards.
Jack Beards!
Harry My father had a small moustache.
Jack A moustache, I've always thought, became a man.
Harry Chamberlain.
Jack Roosevelt.
Harry Schweitzer.
Jack Chaplin.
Harry Hitler . . .
Jack Travel, I've always felt, was a great broadener of the mind.
Harry My word.
Jack Travelled a great deal—when I was young.
Harry Far?
Jack Oh. All over.
Harry A great thing.
Jack Sets its mark upon a man.
Harry Like the army.
Jack Like the army. I suppose the fighting you do has very much the same effect.
Harry Oh, yes.
Jack Bayonet?
Harry What?
Jack The—er.
Harry Oh, bayonet—ball and flame. The old three, we used to call them.
Jack Ah, yes.
Harry A great welder of character.
Jack By Jove.
Harry The youth of today: might have done some good.
Jack Oh, my word, yes.
Harry In the Royal Air Force, of course . . .
Jack Bombs.
Harry Really.
Jack Cannon.

Harry Ah, yes. . . . Couldn't have got far, in our job, I can tell you, without the Royal Air Force.

Jack No. No.

Harry Britannia rules the waves—and rules the skies, too. I shouldn't wonder.

Jack Oh, yes.

Harry Nowadays, of course . . .

Jack Rockets.

Harry Ah, yes.

Jack They say . . .

Harry Yes?

Jack When the next catastrophe occurs . . .

Harry Oh, yes.

Jack The island itself might very well be flooded.

Harry Really.

Jack Except for the more prominent peaks, of course.

Harry Oh, yes.

Jack While we're sitting here waiting to be buried . . .

Harry Oh, yes.

Jack (*laughing*) We'll end up being drowned.

Harry Extraordinary! (*He laughs*) No Vale of Evesham then.

Jack Oh, no.

Harry (*laughing*) Nor your aunt at Gloucester!

Jack She died, you know, a short while ago.

Harry Oh. I am sorry.

Jack We weren't very attached.

Harry Oh, no.

Jack Still. She was a very remarkable woman.

Harry Ah, yes.

Jack In her own particular way. So few characters around these days. So few interesting people.

Harry Oh, yes.

Jack Uniformity.

Harry (*looking off*) Mrs Washington.

Jack Really? I've been keeping an eye open for her. (*Rising*)

Harry Striking woman.

Jack Her husband was related to a distant cousin of mine, on my father's side. (*Straightening his tie, etc*)

Harry My word.

Jack I shouldn't be surprised if she recognizes me . . . No . . .

Harry Scarcely glanced. Her mind on other things.

Jack Oh, yes. (*He sits*)

Harry Spot of cloud there.

Jack (*taking out a coin*) Seen this? There. Nothing up my sleeve. Ready? One, two, three . . . Gone.

Harry My word.

Jack Here. (*Taking out three playing cards*) Pick out the Queen of Hearts

Harry This one.

Jack That's right. Now—Queen of Hearts.
Harry This one.
Jack No!
Harry Oh!

They laugh

Jack Try again. There she is. (*He shuffles them round on the table*) Where is she?
Harry Er . . .
Jack Take your time.
Harry This one . . . Oh!

They laugh

Jack That one!
Harry Well. I'll have to study those.
Jack Easy when you know how. I have some more back there. One of my favourite tricks is to take the ace of spades out of someone's top pocket.
Harry (*looking in his pocket*) Oh . . .
Jack No. No. No. (*He laughs*) It needs some preparation. Sometimes in a lady's handbag. That goes down very well.
Harry Goodness.
Jack I knew a man at one time—a friend of the family, on my father's side —who could put a lighted cigarette into his mouth, take one half from one ear, and the other half from the other.
Harry Goodness.
Jack Still lighted.
Harry How on earth did he do that?
Jack I don't know.
Harry I suppose—physiologically—it's possible then.
Jack Shouldn't think so.
Harry No.
Jack One of the advantages, of course, of sitting here.
Harry Oh, yes.
Jack You can see everyone walking past.
Harry Oh, yes.
Jack Jennings isn't a man I'm awfully fond of.
Harry No.
Jack You've probably noticed yourself.
Harry I have. In the army, I met a man—private—er.
Jack The equivalent rank, of course, in the Air Force, is aircraftsman.
Harry Or able seaman. In the navy.
Jack Able seaman.

They laugh

Harry Goodness.
Jack Funny name. Able seaman. (*He laughs*) I don't think I'd like to be called that.
Harry Yes!

Jack Able seaman! (*He snorts*) One of the great things of course about the war was its feeling of camaraderie.

Harry Friendship.

Jack You found that, too? On the airfield where I was stationed it was really like one great big happy family. My word. The things one did for one another.

Harry Oh, yes.

Jack The way one worked.

Harry Soon passed.

Jack Oh, yes. It did. It did.

Harry Ah, yes.

Jack No sooner was the fighting over than back it came. Back-biting. Complaints. Getting what you can. I sometimes think if the war had been prolonged another thirty years we'd have all felt the benefit.

Harry Oh, yes.

Jack One's children would have grown up far different. That's for sure.

Harry Really? How many have you got?

Jack Two.

Harry Oh, that's very nice.

Jack Boy married. Girl likewise. They seem to rush into things so early these days.

Harry Oh, yes.

Jack And you?

Harry Oh. No. No. Never had the privilege.

Jack Ah, yes. Responsibility. At times you wonder if it's worth it. I had a cousin, on my father's side, who threw herself from a railway carriage.

Harry Oh, dear. How awful.

Jack Yes.

Harry Killed outright.

Jack Well, fortunately, it had just pulled into a station.

Harry I see.

Jack Daughter's married to a salesman. Refrigerators: he sells appliances of that nature.

Harry Oh. Opposite to me.

Jack Yes?

Harry Heating engineer.

Jack Really. I'd never have guessed. How extraordinary.

Harry And yourself?

Jack Oh, I've tinkered with one or two things.

Harry Ah, yes.

Jack What I like about my present job is the scope that it leaves you for initiative.

Harry Rather. Same with mine.

Jack Distribution of foodstuffs in a wholesale store.

Harry Really.

Jack Thinking out new ideas. Constant speculation.

Harry Oh, yes.

Jack Did you know if you put jam into small cardboard containers it will
sell far better than if you put it into large glass jars?

Harry Really?

Jack Psychological. When you buy it in a jar you're wondering what on
earth—subconsciously—you're going to do with the glass bottle. But
with a cardboard box that anxiety is instantly removed. Result: improved
sales: improved production: lower prices: improved distribution.

Harry That's a fascinating job.

Jack Oh, yes. If you use your brains there's absolutely nothing there to
stop you.

Harry I can see.

Jack Heating must be a very similar problem.

Harry Oh, yes.

Jack The different ways of warming up a house.

Harry Yes.

Jack Or not warming it up, as the case may be.

Harry Yes!

They laugh

Jack I don't think I've met your wife.

Harry No. No. . . . As a matter of fact. We've been separated for a little
while.

Jack Oh, dear.

Harry One of those misfortunes.

Jack Happens a great deal.

Harry Oh, yes.

Jack Each have our cross.

Harry Oh, yes.

Jack Well. Soon be time for lunch.

Harry Will. And I haven't had my walk.

Jack No. Still.

Harry Probably do as much good.

Jack Oh, yes.

Harry (*rising*) Well, then . . .

Jack (*pointing to the newspaper*) Yours or mine?

Harry (*picking up the newspaper*) Mine, I believe.

Jack (*rising*) Ah, yes.

Harry Very fine gloves.

Jack Yes.

Harry Pacamac.

Jack All correct.

Harry Cane.

Jack Cane.

Harry Well, then. Off we go.

Jack Off we go.

Harry (*pausing*) Beautiful corner.

Jack 'Tis.

Harry Work up an appetite.

Jack Right, then. Best foot forward.
Harry Best foot forward.
Jack Best foot forward, and off we go.

Jack and Harry stroll off down L *as the lights darken to a half-light, then come up on—*

SCENE 2

Kathleen and Marjorie come on up R.

Kathleen is a stout middle-aged lady; she wears a coat which is unbuttoned, a headscarf, and strap shoes. She is limping, supported by Marjorie. Marjorie is also middle-aged. She is dressed in a skirt and cardigan. She carries an umbrella and a large, well-used bag.

Kathleen Gawd. Cor—*blimey! (She limps to the chair* R, *sits down and holds her foot)*
Marjorie Going to rain, ask me.
Kathleen Rain all it wants, ask me. Cor—*blimey!* Going to kill me is this.
Marjorie Going to rain and catch us out here. That's what it's going to do. *(She puts her umbrella up, worn, and moves* R)
Kathleen Going to rain all right, in't it? Going to rain all right. Put your umbrella up. Sun's still shining. Cor blimey. Invite rain that will. Common sense, girl . . . *(She massages her foot)*
Marjorie *(crossing* L) Out here and no shelter. Be all right if it starts.
Kathleen Cor blimey! My bleeding feet . . . surprise me they don't drop off—cut clean through these will . . .
Marjorie Clouds all over. Told you we shouldn't have come out.
Kathleen Get nothing if you don't try, girl. Cor *blimey!*
Marjorie I don't know.
Kathleen Here. You'll be all right, won't you?

Marjorie looks at her enquiringly

   Holes there is. See right through, you can.
Marjorie What?
Kathleen Here. Rain come straight through that. Won't get much shelter under that. What d'I tell you? Might as well sit under a shower. *(She laughs)* Cor blimey. You'll be all right, won't you?
Marjorie Be all right with you in any case. Walk no faster than a snail.
Kathleen Not surprised. Don't want me to escape. That's my trouble, girl.
Marjorie Here . . . *(She sits)*

Jack and Harry enter up L, *slowly pass across and exit up* R

Kathleen What've we got for lunch?
Marjorie Sprouts.
Kathleen Seen them have you? *(She massages her foot)*

Marjorie Smelled 'em!
Kathleen What's today, then?
Marjorie Friday.
Kathleen End of week.
Marjorie Corn' beef hash.
Kathleen That's Wednesday.
Marjorie Sausage roll.
Kathleen Think you're right. Cor *blimey*. (*She groans and holds her foot*)
Marjorie Know what you ought to do, don't you? Ask for another pair of shoes, girl, you ask me.
Kathleen Took me laced ones, haven't they? Only ones that fitted. Thought I'd hang myself, didn't they? Only five inches long.
Marjorie What they think you are?
Kathleen Bleedin' mouse, more likely.
Marjorie Here. Not like the last one I was in.
Kathleen No?
Marjorie Let you paint on the walls they did. Do anyfing. Just muck around. Here—I won't tell you what some of them did.
Kathleen What?

Marjorie leans over and whispers

Never.
Marjorie Cross me heart.
Kathleen Glad I wasn't there. This place is bad enough. You seen Henderson, have you?
Marjorie Ought to lock him up you ask me.
Kathleen What d'you do then?
Marjorie Here?
Kathleen At this other place.
Marjorie Noffing. Mucked around . . .
Kathleen Here . . .

Jack and Harry stroll across again, slowly, from up R, *in conversation: heads back, deep breathing, bracing arms, etc. The women wait for them to exit up* L

Marjorie My dentist comes from Pakistan.
Kathleen Yours?
Marjorie Took out all me teeth.
Kathleen Those not your own, then?
Marjorie All went rotten when I had my little girl. There she is, waitress at the seaside.
Kathleen And you stuck here . . .
Marjorie No teeth . . .
Kathleen Don't appreciate it.
Marjorie They don't.
Kathleen Never.

Marjorie Might take this down if it doesn't rain.
Kathleen Cor blimey—take these off if I thought I could get 'em on again (*She groans*) Tried catching a serious disease.
Marjorie When was that?
Kathleen Only had me in two days. Said, nothing the matter with you, my girl.
Marjorie Don't believe you.
Kathleen Next thing: got home: smashed everything in sight.
Marjorie No?
Kathleen Winders. Cooker. Nearly broke me back. Thought I'd save the telly. Still owed eighteen months. Thought: 'Everything or nothing, girl . . .'
Marjorie Rotten programmes. (*She takes down her umbrella*)
Kathleen Didn't half give it a good old conk. (*She laughs*)
Marjorie There's one thing. You get a good night's sleep.
Kathleen Like being with a steam engine, where I come from. Cor blimey, that much whistling and groaning: think you're going to take off.
Marjorie More like a boa-constrictor, ask me. Here . . .

Jack and Harry stroll across again from up L, *still taking the air, etc. and exit up* R

Started crying everywhere I went. Started off on Christmas Eve.
Kathleen S'happy time, Christmas.
Marjorie Didn't stop till Boxing Day.
Kathleen If He ever comes again I hope He comes on Whit Tuesday. For me that's the best time of the year.
Marjorie Why's that?
Kathleen Dunno. Whit Tuesday's always been a lucky day for me. First party I ever went to was on a Whit Tuesday. First feller I went with. Can't be the date. Different every year.
Marjorie My lucky day's the last Friday in any month with an "r" in it when the next month doesn't begin later than the following Monday.
Kathleen How do you make that out?
Marjorie Dunno. I was telling the doctor that the other day . . . (*She looks off*) There's that man with the binoculars watching you.
Kathleen Where?
Marjorie Lift your dress up.
Kathleen No.
Marjorie Go on. (*She leans over and lifts Kathleen's dress*) Told you . .
Kathleen Looks like he's got diarrhoea! (*They laugh*) See that chap the other day? Showed his slides of a trip up the Amazon River.
Marjorie See that one with no clothes on? Supposed to be cooking his dinner.
Kathleen Won't have him here again . . .
Marjorie Showing all his p's and q's.
Kathleen Ooooooh! (*She screeches, covering her mouth*)
Marjorie Here . . .

Jack and Harry stroll back down R, *glancing over now at Marjorie and Kathleen, and exit up* L

Kathleen Lord and Lady used to live here at one time. (*Glancing after Harry*)
Marjorie Who's that?
Kathleen Dunno.
Marjorie Probably still inside, ask me. (*She laughs*) See that woman with dyed hair? Told me she'd been in films. "What films?" I said. "Blue Films?"
Kathleen What she say?
Marjorie "The ones I was in was not in colour." (*They laugh*) I s'll lose me teeth one of these days—oooh!
Kathleen Better'n losing something else . . .
Marjorie Ooooh! (*She screeches*) Here . . .

Jack and Harry stroll back on up L, *and cross down* R

Jack Good day, ladies. (*He raises his hat*)
Kathleen Good day yourself, your lordships.
Jack Oh, now. I wouldn't go as far as that.
Harry No. No. Still a bit of the common touch.
Jack Least, so I'd hope.
Harry Oh, yes.
Marjorie And how have you been keeping, professor?
Jack Professor? I can see we're a little elevated today.
Marjorie Don't know about elevated. But *we're* sitting down.

Kathleen and Marjorie laugh

Kathleen Been standing up, we have, for hours.
Harry Hours?
Marjorie When you were sitting down.
Jack Oh dear—I wasn't aware . . .
Kathleen 'Course you were. My bleedin' feet. Just look at them. (*She holds her feet again*)
Marjorie Pull your skirt down, girl.
Kathleen Oh, Gawd . . .
Jack My friend here, Harry, is a specialist in housewarming, and I myself am a retailer in preserves.
Marjorie Ooooh! (*To Kathleen*) What did I tell you?
Kathleen No atomic bombs today?
Jack No. no. Shouldn't think so. (*Looking up*)
Marjorie And how's your mongol sister?
Harry Mongol . . .? I'm afraid you must have the wrong person, Ma'm.
Kathleen Ooooh!
Jack My friend, I'm afraid, is separated from his wife. As a consequence, I can assure you, of many hardships . . .
Marjorie Of course . . .
Jack And I myself, though happily married in some respects, would not pretend that my situation is all it should be . . .

Kathleen Ooooh!

Jack One endeavours—but it is in the nature of things, I believe, that, on the whole one fails.

Kathleen Ooooh!

Harry My friend, Jack, has invented several new methods of retailing jam.

Kathleen Ooooh!

Marjorie Jam. I like that.

Jack Really?

Marjorie Strawberry. My favourite.

Kathleen Raspberry, mine.

Marjorie Ooooh!

Jack A friend of mine, on my father's side, once owned a small factory which was given over, exclusively, to its manufacture.

Kathleen Ooooh!

Jack In very large vats.

Kathleen Ooooh!

Marjorie I like treacle myself.

Jack Treacle, now, is a very different matter.

Marjorie Comes from Malaya.

Harry That's rubber, I believe. (*He has crossed up* C)

Marjorie In tins.

Harry The rubber comes from Malaya, I believe.

Marjorie I eat it, don't I? I ought to know.

Kathleen She has treacle on her bread.

Jack I believe it comes, as a matter of fact, from the West Indies.

Kathleen West Indies? Where's that?

Marjorie Near Hong Kong.

Harry That's the East Indies, I believe.

Marjorie You ever been to the North Indies?

Harry I don't believe . . .

Marjorie Well, that's where treacle comes from.

Harry I see . . .

There is a pause

Jack We were just remarking, as a matter of fact, that Mrs Glover isn't looking her usual self.

Kathleen Who's she?

Jack The lady with the rather embarrassing disfigurement . . .

Marjorie Her with one ear?

Kathleen The one who's only half a nose.

Marjorie She snores.

Kathleen You'd snore as well, wouldn't you, if you only had half a nose.

Marjorie Eaten away.

Kathleen What?

Marjorie Her husband ate it one night when she was sleeping.

Kathleen Silly to fall asleep with any man, I say. These days they get up to anything. Read it in the papers an' next thing they want to try it themselves.

Jack Public morality, I agree, is not all it should be.
Harry The weather's been particularly mild today.
Kathleen Not like my flaming feet. Oooh . . .
Jack As one grows older these little things are sent to try us.
Kathleen Little? Cor blimey: I take size seven.
Harry My word.
Marjorie He wishes he was sitting in this chair, doesn't he?
Harry What . . .
Jack It's extraordinary that more facilities of this nature aren't supplied, in my view.
Kathleen Only bit of garden with any flowers. Half-a-dozen daisies . . .
Harry Tulips . . .
Jack Roses . . .
Kathleen I know daisies, don't I? Those are daisies. Grow three feet tall.
Harry Really? (*He moves down* L)
Marjorie Rest of it's all covered in muck.
Jack Oh, now. Not as bad as that.
Marjorie What? I call that muck. What's it supposed to be?
Harry A rockery, I believe.
Kathleen Rockery? More like a rubbish tip ask me.
Jack Probably the flowers haven't grown yet.
Marjorie Flowers? How do you grow flowers on old bricks and bits of plaster?
Harry Certain categories, of course . . .
Jack Oh, yes.
Harry Can be trained to grow in these conditions. (*He crosses down* R)
Kathleen You're round the bend, you are. Ought to have you up there, they did.
Harry (*to Jack*) They tell me the flowers are just as bad at that end, too.

Harry and Jack laugh at their private joke, down R

Marjorie If you ask me all this is just typical.
Jack Typical?
Marjorie One table. Two chairs—between one thousand people.
Kathleen Two, they tell me.
Marjorie Two thousand. One thousand for this chair, and one thousand for that.
Harry There are, of course, the various benches.
Kathleen Benches? Seen better sold for firewood.
Marjorie Make red marks they do across your bum.
Kathleen Ooooh! (*She screeches*)
Harry Clouding slightly.
Jack Slightly.
Marjorie Pull your skirt down, girl.
Kathleen Ooooh!
Harry Of course, one alternative would be to bring, say, a couple of more chairs out with us.
Jack Oh, yes. Now that would be a solution.

Harry Four chairs. One each. I don't believe, say, for an afternoon they'd be missed from the lecture hall.

Marjorie Here, you see *Up the Amazon* last night?

Jack Tuesday . . .

Harry Tuesday.

Jack Believe I did, now you mention it.

Marjorie See that feller with a loincloth?

Kathleen Ooooh!

Jack I must admit, there are certain attractions in the primitive life.

Kathleen Ooooh!

Jack Air, space . . .

Marjorie Seen all he's got, that's all you seen.

Jack I believe there was a moment when the eye . . .

Kathleen Moment—ooooh!

Harry I thought his pancakes looked rather nice.

Kathleen Ooooh!

Harry On the little log . . .

Kathleen Ooooh!

Marjorie Not his pancakes he's seen, my girl.

Kathleen Ooooh!

Jack The canoe, now, was not unlike my own little boat.

Kathleen Ooooh!

Harry Fishing there somewhat more than a mere pastime.

Jack Oh, yes.

Harry Life and death.

Jack Oh, yes.

Marjorie Were you the feller they caught climbing out of a window here last week?

Jack Me?

Marjorie Him.

Harry Don't think so. Don't recollect that?

Jack Where, if you don't mind me asking, did you acquire that information?

Marjorie Where? (*To Kathleen*) Here, I thought you told me it was him.

Kathleen Not me. Mrs Heller.

Marjorie You sure?

Kathleen Not me, anyway.

Jack I had a relative—nephew as a matter of fact, who started a window-cleaning business—let me see—three years ago now.

Harry Really?

Jack Great scope there for an adventurous man.

Marjorie In bathroom windows specially.

Kathleen Ooooh!

Jack Heights—distances . . .

Harry On very tall buildings, of course, they lower them from the roof. (*He crosses down* L)

Jack Oh, yes.

Harry Don't have the ladders long enough, you know.

Kathleen Ooooh!

Jack Your friend seems in a very jovial frame of mind.

Harry Like to see that.

Jack Oh, yes. Gloom: one sees it far too much in this place. Mr Metcalf, now: I don't think he's spoken to anyone since the day that he arrived.

Marjorie What's he, then?

Harry He's the gentleman who's constantly pacing up and down.

Jack One says hello, of course. He scarcely seems to notice.

Kathleen Wasn't one of you a qualified doctor at one time?

Harry Qualified?

Jack There was a short period when I did submit as it were, to medical tuition. As it turned out, however, with the modest circumstances of my family, I was obliged in the end to discontinue. I have a cousin, however, who is actually in the profession . . .

Harry And an aunt . . .

Jack Of course. Of course.

Kathleen Hear you were asking if they'd let you out.

Jack Who?

Marjorie Your friend.

Harry Oh. Nothing as dramatic—certain enquiries—temporary visit—domestic problems, you know. Without a man very little, I'm afraid, gets done.

Marjorie It gets too much done, if you ask me. That's half the trouble.

Kathleen Oooooh!

Harry However, it seems that certain aspects of it can be cleared up by correspondence. One doesn't wish, after all, to impose unduly . . .

Jack Oh, no.

Harry Events have their own momentum. Take their time.

Marjorie You married to me, they would. I can tell you.

Kathleen Oooooh!

Harry Oh, now, Missis—er . . .

Marjorie Madam.

Kathleen Ooooh!

Harry Well—er—that might be a situation that could well be beneficial to us both, in different circumstances, in different places . . .

Jack Quite . . .

Marjorie Listen to him!

Harry We all have our little foibles, our little failings.

Jack Oh, indeed.

Harry Hardly be human without.

Jack Oh, no.

Harry The essence of true friendship, in my view, is to make allowances for one another's little lapses.

Marjorie Heard all about your little lapses, haven't we?

Kathleen Ooooooooh!

Jack All have our little falls from grace.

Marjorie Burn down the whole bleedin' building, he will. Given up smoking because they won't let him have any matches.

Kathleen Oooh!

Jack The rumours that drift around a place like this—hardly worth the trouble . . .

Harry Absolutely. (*He crosses down* R)

Jack If one believed everything one heard . . .

Harry Oh, yes.

Jack I was remarking to my friend earlier this morning: if one can't enjoy life as it takes one, what's the point of living it at all? One can't, after all, spend the whole of one's life inside a shell.

Harry Oh, no.

Marjorie Know what he'd spend it inside if he had half a chance.

Kathleen Oooooh!

Marjorie Tell my husband of you, I shall.

Kathleen Bus-driver.

Jack Really? I've taken a life-long interest in public transport.

Kathleen Oooh!

Marjorie Taken a life-long interest in something else more'n likely.

Kathleen Oooooh!

Jack I was saying to my companion this morning, travel is a great broadener of the mind. Opening vistas.

Marjorie Pull your skirt down, girl!

Kathleen Oooooh!

Marjorie Know his kind.

Kathleen Oooooh!

Jack Respect for the gentler sex, I must say, is a fast diminishing concept in the modern world.

Harry Oh, yes.

Jack I recollect the time when one stood for a lady as a matter of course.

Harry Oh, yes.

Marjorie Know the kind of standing he's on about.

Kathleen Oooooh!

Jack Each becomes hardened to his ways.

Kathleen Oooooooh!

Jack No regard for anyone else's.

Marjorie Be missing your dinner, you will. Here. Are you all right?

Jack (*beginning to cry, vaguely*) Slight moment of discomposure . . . (*He takes out his handkerchief and wipes his eyes*)

Harry My friend is a man—he won't mind me saying this . . .

Jack No—no . . .

Harry Of great sensibility and feeling.

Kathleen Here, You having us on?

Jack I assure you, madam—I regret any anxiety, or concern which I may, unwittingly, have caused. In fact—I'm sure my friend will concur—perhaps you'll allow us to accompany you to the dining-hall. I have noticed, in the past, that though one has to queue, to leave it any later is to run the risk of being served with a cold plate: the food cold and, the manners of the cook—at times, I must confess—appalling. (*Moving* RC)

Kathleen (*to Marjorie*) We'll have to go. There'll be nothing left.
Marjorie It's this seat he's after.
Harry I assure you, madam—we are on our way.
Kathleen (*to Harry*) Here: you mind if I lean on your arm?
Marjorie Kathleen!
Harry Oh, now. That's a very pretty name.
Kathleen Got straps—make your ankles swell. (*She rises*)
Harry (*holding out his arm*) Allow me.
Kathleen (*taking it*) Oh. Thank you.
Harry Harry.
Kathleen Harry.
Harry And this is my friend—Jack.
Kathleen Jack. And this is my friend Marjorie.
Jack Marjorie. Delightful.
Marjorie Here, you all right?
Kathleen You carrying it with you, or are you coming?
Jack Allow me . . .
Marjorie Here . . . (*She rises quickly*)
Jack Marjorie . . .
Harry Perhaps after lunch we might meet here again.
Jack A little chat. Time passes very slowly.
Marjorie Here, where's my bag?
Kathleen Need carrying out, I will.
Harry Now, then. All right.
Kathleen Have you all the time, I shall.
Harry Ready? All aboard then are we?
Marjorie Well, then. All right . . . (*She takes Jack's arm,* R)
Jack Right then. Dining-hall—here we come!
Harry Sausages today, if I'm not mistaken. (*He starts to move off*)
Kathleen Ooooh!
Marjorie Corned beef hash.
Kathleen Ooooh!
Jack One as good as another, I always say.
Kathleen Oooooh!
Harry Turned out better.
Jack Turned out better.
Harry Altogether.
Jack Altogether.
Harry Well, then. Here we go.

They all go off up L

The CURTAIN *falls*

ACT II

The stage lightens

Alfred is standing up C, *a large, well-made young man: shirt, but no tie. He looks* L, *looks* R, *sees the table, comes down* C. *He walks past the table, slowly eyeing it. He pauses, glances back at it from* R. *He comes back, watching the table rather furtively, sideways, moving* L. *He pauses, his hands behind his back. Suddenly he leaps at the table; grasps it; struggles with it as if it had a life of its own. He groans, struggles. Finally he lifts the table above his head.*

Marjorie comes up R: *umbrella furled*

Marjorie   Here. You all right? (*She comes down* R)
Alfred What?
Marjorie Alfred, i'n it?
Alfred Yeh. (*He still holds the table above his head*)
Marjorie You'll break that, you will.
Alfred Yeh . . .
Marjorie You seen my mate? (*Looking round*)

Alfred looks at her enquiringly

Marjorie Woman that limps.
Alfred No.
Marjorie One day you get seconds and they go off without you. You like treacle pud?
Alfred Yeh.
Marjorie Get seconds?
Alfred No.
Marjorie Shoulda waited.
Alfred Yeh.
Marjorie Said they'd be out here after "Remedials".

Alfred looks at her enquiringly

Marjorie You do Remedials?
Alfred Yeh.
Marjorie What 'you do?
Alfred Baskets.
Marjorie Baskets. Shoulda known.
Alfred You got sixpence.
Marjorie No. Better go find her. Let anybody turn them round her hand, she will.
Alfred Yeh.

Marjorie goes off down L.

Alfred lowers the table slowly, almost like a ritual. He crouches, picks up one chair by a leg and lifts it, exaggerating the effort, etc. He stands, slowly, as he gets it up. He bends his arm slowly; lifts the chair above his head. He puts it down. He stands a moment, gazing down at the two chairs and the table sideways. He walks round them; then walks round them again, a little farther R. *Then he grabs the second chair. and lifts it, one-handed, like the first chair, but more quickly. He lifts it above his head; begins to wrestle with it as if it too possessed a life of its own, his grip, however, still one-handed.*

Marjorie comes on up L; *pauses, looks over, then goes off up* L

Alfred does not see her. He struggles, overcomes the chair, almost absent-mindedly lowers it, looks L, *looks* R, *puts the chair beneath his arm and goes down* R

Kathleen limps on up R, *followed by Harry carrying a wicker chair*

Kathleen Nah, this side's better. Oh . . .
Harry Oh. Look at that.
Kathleen Where's the other one gone, then?
Harry Well, that's a damned nuisance.
Kathleen Still only two. Don't know what they'll say. (*She comes down* C)
Harry Oh, dear.
Kathleen Pinch anything round here. Can't turn you back. Gawd . . .! (*She sits on the metal chair as Harry holds it*)
Harry There, now.
Kathleen Good to get off your feet . . .
Harry Yes, well . . . (*He sets his own chair down, turning it one way then another*)
Kathleen Better sit on it. No good standing about. Don't know where she's got to. Where's your friend looking?
Harry Went to Remedials, I believe. (*He sits*)
Kathleen Get you in there won't let you out again. Here—he really what he says he is?
Harry How do you mean?
Kathleen Told us he was a doctor. Another time he said he'd been a sanitary inspector.
Harry Really? Hadn't heard of that.
Kathleen Go on. Know what inspecting he'll do. You the same.
Harry Oh, now. Certain discriminations can be . . .
Kathleen I've heard about you.
Harry Oh, well, you er.
Kathleen Making up things.
Harry Oh, well. One—embodies—of course.
Kathleen What's that then?
Harry Fancies. What's life for if you can't . . . (*He flutters his fingers*)
Kathleen (*imitating Harry's action*) We've heard about that an' all.

Harry Well. I'm sure you and I have, in reality, a great deal in common. After all, one looks around: what does one see?

Kathleen Gawd . . . (*She groans, feeling her feet*)

Harry A little this. A little that.

Katheen Here. Everything you know is little.

Harry Well, I—er—yes. No great role for this actor, I'm afraid. A little stage, a tiny part.

Kathleen You an actor then?

Harry Well, I did, as a matter of fact, at one time—actually, a little . . .

Kathleen Here, little again. You notice?

Harry Oh . . . you're right.

Kathleen What parts you play, then?

Harry Well, as a matter of fact—not your Hamlets, of course, your Ophelias: more the little bystander who passes by the . . .

Kathleen Here. Little.

Harry Oh—yes! (*He laughs*)

Kathleen Play anything romantic?

Harry Oh, romance, now, was—never very far away.

Kathleen Here . . .

Harry One was cast, of course—

Kathleen Think I could have been romantic.

Harry Oh, yes.

Kathleen Had the chance. Got it here. (*She clasps her heart*)

Harry Oh, yes . . .

Kathleen Had different shoes than this . . .

Harry Oh, yes—everything, of course, provided . . .

Kathleen Going to be a commotion, you ask me . . .

Harry Commotion . . .?

Kathleen When they get here. Three chairs—if he brings one as well. He'll have to stand. (*She laughs*)

Harry Could have been confiscated, you know.

Kathleen Confiscated?

Harry Often happens. See a little pleasure and down they come.

Kathleen Here—little.

Harry Goodness . . . yes. (*He pauses*) One of the advantages of this spot, you know, is that it catches the sun so nicely.

Kathleen What bit there is of it.

Harry Bit?

Kathleen All that soot. Cuts it down. 'Stead of browning you turns you black.

Harry Black?

Kathleen All over.

Harry An industrial nation . . .

Kathleen Gawd . . . (*She eases her feet*)

Harry Can't have the benefit of both. Nature as well as er . . . The one is incurred at the expense of the other.

Kathleen Your friend come in for following little girls?

Harry What . . .

Kathleen Go on. You can tell me. Cross me heart and hope to die.

Harry Well—that's . . .

Kathleen Well, then.

Harry I believe there were—er—certain proclivities, shall we say?

Kathleen Proclivities? What's them?

Harry Nothing criminal, of course.

Kathleen Oh, no . . .

Harry No prosecution . . .

Kathleen Oh, no . . .

Harry Certain pressures, in the er—revealed themselves.

Kathleen In public?

Harry No. No—I—not what I meant.

Kathleen I don't know what you're saying half the time. You realize that?

Harry Communication is a difficult factor.

Kathleen Say that again.

Harry I believe he was encouraged to come here for a little, er. . . .

Kathleen Here. Little.

Harry Oh, yes. As it is, very few places left now where one can be at ease.

Kathleen Could go on his holidays. Seaside.

Harry Beaches? Crowded all the while.

Kathleen Could go to the country.

Harry Spaces . . .

Kathleen Sent me to the country once. All them trees. Worse'n people. Gawd. Take them off if I thought I could get them on again. Can't understand why they don't let me have me laces. Took me belt as well. Who they think I'm going to strangle? Improved my figure, it did, the belt. Drew it in a bit.

Harry Oh, now, I would say, myself, the proportions were in reasonable condition.

Kathleen Oh, now . . .

Harry Without, of course, wishing to seem immodest . . .

Kathleen Get little enough encouragement in my life. Gawd . . . My friend, you know, was always crying.

Harry Oh, now.

Kathleen Everywhere she went—cigarettes. No sooner in the shop, opens her mouth, and out it comes. Same on buses.

Harry Oh, dear, now.

Kathleen Doesn't like sympathy.

Harry Ah, yes.

Kathleen Get all I can myself.

Harry Husband a bus-driver, I believe.

Kathleen Hers. Not mine.

Harry Ah, yes.

Kathleen Mine's a corporation employee.

Harry Ah, yes. One of the . . .

Kathleen Cleans up muck. Whenever there's a pile of muck they send him to clean it up.

Harry I see.

Kathleen You worked in a bank, then?

Harry Well, in a er.

Kathleen Clean job. Don't know why he doesn't get a clean job. Door-man. Smells awful, he does. Gets bathed one night and the next day just the same.

Harry Ah, yes.

Kathleen Puts you off your food.

Harry Yes.

Kathleen "They ought to fumigate you", I said.

Harry Yes?

Kathleen Know what he says?

Harry Yes?

Kathleen "Ought to fumigate you, my girl, and forget to switch it orf."

Harry Goodness.

Kathleen It's going to be tea-time before they get here.

Harry (*examining his watch*) No, no. Still a little time.

Kathleen Your wife alive?

Harry Er.

Kathleen Separated?

Harry Well, I . . .

Kathleen Unsympathetic.

Harry Yes?

Kathleen Your wife.

Harry Well—one can ask too much these days, I believe, of er.

Kathleen Met once a fortnight wouldn't be any divorce. Ridiculous, living together. S'not human.

Harry No . . .

Kathleen Like animals. Even they run off when they're not feeling like it.

Harry Oh, yes.

Kathleen Not natural. One man. One woman. Who's He think He is?

Harry looks round

No—Him. (*She points up*)

Harry Oh, yes . . .

Kathleen Made Him a bachelor. Cor blimey: no wife for Him.

Harry No.

Kathleen Saved somebody the trouble.

Harry Yes.

Kathleen Does it all by telepathy.

Harry Yes.

Kathleen Kids?

Harry What? Oh. No.

Kathleen Got married how old?

Harry Twenty er.

Kathleen Man shouldn't marry till he's forty. Ridiculous. Don't know what they want till then. After that, too old to bother.

Harry Oh, yes.

Kathleen Here . . .

Alfred comes in down R *carrying the chair. He sees the others, nods then returns the way he came*

Here! That's where it's gone.
Harry Don't believe . . .
Kathleen That's Alfred.
Harry Yes?
Kathleen Wrestler.
Harry Yes.
Kathleen Up here. (*She taps her head*)
Harry Oh.
Kathleen Where you going when you leave here?
Harry Well—I—er.
Kathleen Lost your job?
Harry Well, I . . .
Kathleen Wife not have you?
Harry Well I . . .
Kathleen Another man.
Harry Oh, now . . .
Kathleen Still, could be worse.
Harry Oh, yes.
Kathleen What's he want with that, then? Here, you were slow to ask.
Harry Yes . . .
Kathleen You all right?
Harry Touch of the . . . (*He wipes his eyes*)
Kathleen Here, couple of old cry babies you are. Bad as my friend.
Harry Yes, well . . .
Kathleen Shoot my brains out if I had a chance. Gawd! Tried to kill myself with gas.
Harry Yes . . .?
Kathleen Kiddies at my sister's. Head in oven. Knock on door. Milkman. Two weeks behind, he said. Broke everything, I did.
Harry Yes?
Kathleen Nearly killed him. Would, too, if I could have got hold. Won't tap on our door, I can tell you. Not again.
Harry Goodness.
Kathleen You all right?
Harry Yes—I—er.
Kathleen Here. Hold my hand if you like.
Harry Oh, now.
Kathleen Here. (*She puts her hand on the table*) Not much to look at.
Harry Oh, now. I wouldn't say that.
Kathleen Go on.
Harry Well, I . . . (*He takes her hand*)
Kathleen Our age: know what it's all about.
Harry Oh, well. A long road, you know.
Kathleen Can't get to old age fast enough for me. Sooner they put me under . . .

Harry Oh, now . . .
Kathleen Different for a man.
Harry Well, I . . .
Kathleen I know. Have your troubles. Still. Woman's different.
Harry Oh, I . . .
Kathleen Wouldn't be a woman. Not again . . . Here!

Alfred enters up R, *carrying the chair. He crosses, pausing as Kathleen calls, then exits up* L

Been here years, you know. Do the work of ten men if they set him to it.
Harry (*looking off*) I say . . .
Kathleen Dunno where they've been. Oi! Deaf as a post. Here, no need to let go. Think you're shy.
Harry Oh, well . . .
Kathleen Never mind. Too old to be disappointed.
Harry Oh, now . . .

Jack and Marjorie enter, up R, *Jack carrying a wicker chair, and come down* C

Marjorie Here you are, then. Been looking for you all over.
Kathleen Been here, haven't we, all the time.

Harry stands

Jack Sun still strong.
Harry Oh, yes. (*He moves down* R)
Marjorie Here. Where's the other chair?
Kathleen He's taken it over there.
Marjorie What's he doing?
Kathleen Dunno. Here, sit on his knee if you want to!
Marjorie Catch me. Who do you think I am? (*She sits*)
Kathleen Well, no good you both standing.
Jack (*To Harry*) No, no. After you, old man.
Harry No, no. After you . . .
Kathleen Be here all day, you ask me. Here, I'll stand. Gawd . . .
Jack Oh, no . . .
Harry Ridiculous.
Kathleen Oh, gawd!
Marjorie Take it in turns.
Jack Right, I'll er.
Harry Do. Do. Go ahead.
Jack Oh, that's very—very. (*He sits*)
Marjorie Been carrying that around, looking for you, he has.
Kathleen Been here, we have, all the time.
Marjorie What you been up to, then?
Kathleen Nothing you might mind.
Marjorie (*to Harry*) Want to watch her. Men all the time.

Kathleen One who knows.

Marjorie Seen it with my own eyes.

Kathleen Lot more besides.

Jack Well, looking up, shouldn't wonder. Clearing . . . (*Gazing up*)

Harry Oh. Very.

Marjorie Fallen in love, she has.

Jack Damn nuisance about the chair, what?

Harry Oh. Very.

Marjorie Has to see the doctor about it, she has.

Kathleen See the doctor about you, girl.

Marjorie Can't let no tradesman near the house. Five kids. Milkman, window-cleaner . . .

Kathleen Know your trouble, don't you?

Marjorie Nothing's bad as yours.

Kathleen Can't go down the street without her trousers wetting.

Jack Spot more sun, see those flowers out. Shouldn't wonder.

Harry Oh, yes.

Jack By Jove, Farrer, isn't it? (*Looking off* L)

Harry Say he was a champion quarter-miler.

Jack Shouldn't wonder. Build of an athlete. Square shoulders.

Harry Deep chest.

Jack Oh, yes.

Kathleen You know what you should do with your mouth, girl.

Marjorie You know what you should do with something else.

Kathleen Oh . . . (*To Harry*) Take a little stroll if you don't mind . . . Gawd strewth! (*She rises*)

Harry hastens to take Kathleen's arm

Marjorie Mind she doesn't stroll you to the bushes.

Kathleen (*crossing down* R *on Harry's arm*) Mind she doesn't splash.

Marjorie See the doctor about you, my girl!

Kathleen See him all the time: your trouble. Not right in the head.

Kathleen and Harry go off down R

Marjorie Can't keep away from men.

Jack Oh, dear. (*Gazing after them*)

Marjorie Gardens.

Jack Oh.

Marjorie Parks especially.

Jack I have heard of such er.

Marjorie Complaints. Used to send the police in threes. Can't trust two and one was never enough.

Jack My word.

Marjorie Oh, yes.

Jack Well, you can never tell a leopard . . .

Marjorie What? Should see her. Spots all over.

Jack Oh, dear.

Marjorie Never washes.
Jack One of the advantages of a late lunch, of course, is that it leaves a shorter space to tea.
Marjorie What's your friend's name?
Jack Harry . . .
Marjorie What's he do, then?
Jack Temporary er. Thought a slight.
Marjorie Get one with her all right. Have another.
Jack Oh, yes . . .
Marjorie Don't know what we're coming to.
Jack Life—mystery . . . (*He gazes up*)

Marjorie watches him. Then—

Marjorie What you put away for, then?
Jack Oh—what?
Marjorie In here.
Jack Oh—little . . .
Marjorie Girl?
Jack Girl?
Marjorie Girls.
Jack Girls?
Marjorie In the street.
Jack Really? (*He looks round*)
Marjorie Here—what you in for?
Jack A wholly voluntary basis, I assure you.
Marjorie Wife put you away?
Jack Oh, no. No, no. Just a moment—needed—thought I might . . .
Marjorie Ever been in the padded whatsit?
Jack Don't believe . . . (*Looking round*)
Marjorie Here—don't tell my friend.
Jack Oh, well . . .
Marjorie Lie there for hours, you can.
Jack Oh, now.
Marjorie Been here twice before.
Jack Really.
Marjorie Don't tell my friend.
Jack Oh, no.
Marjorie Thinks it's my first.
Jack Goodness . . .
Marjorie One of the regulars. Wouldn't know what to do without me.
Jack Oh, yes. Familiar faces.
Marjorie Come for three months: out again. Back again at Christmas.
Jack Oh, yes.
Marjorie Can't stand Christmas.
Jack No. Well. Season of festivities—good cheer.
Marjorie Most people don't talk to you in here. You noticed?
Jack Very rare. Well—find someone to communicate.
Marjorie 'Course. Privileged.

Jack Yes?
Marjorie Being in the reception wing.
Jack Oh, yes.
Marjorie Good as cured.
Jack Oh, yes.
Marjorie Soon be out.
Jack Oh, goodness. Hardly worth the trouble.
Marjorie No.
Jack Home tomorrow!
Marjorie You been married long?
Jack Oh, yes. What?
Marjorie You in love?
Jack What?
Marjorie Your wife.
Jack Clouds. This morning, my friend was remarking on the edges.
Marjorie Hardly worth the trouble.
Jack Oh, yes.
Marjorie Going home.
Jack Oh, well—one has one's—thought I might plant some seeds. Soil not too good I notice . . .
Marjorie Tell you something?
Jack Oh, yes.
Marjorie Set up here for good.
Jack Oh, yes.
Marjorie Here, you listening? What you in for?
Jack Oh . . .
Marjorie Here: you always crying.
Jack Light . . . eye . . . (*He wipes his eye with his handkerchief*)
Marjorie Tell you something.
Jack Yes.
Marjorie Not leave here again.
Jack Oh, no.

> *There is a pause, then Alfred comes on up* L, *still carrying the chair. He pauses up* C

Marjorie You going to sit on that or something?
Alfred What?
Marjorie Sit.
Alfed Dunno. (*He comes down* R *then pauses*)
Marjorie Give it to somebody who can, you do.
Alfred What?
Marjorie Give it to somebody who can.
Alfred Yeh.
Marjorie You know my friend?
Alfred No.
Marjorie This is Alfred.
Jack (*standing formally*) Oh—good day.

Alfred Where you get your cane?
Jack Oh—came with me. (*He looks down at it*)
Alfred I had a cane like that once.
Jack Ah, yes.
Alfred Nicked it.
Jack Oh, now.
Marjorie Had it when he came. Didn't you. Sit down.
Jack Yes. (*He sits*)
Alfred Wanna fight?
Jack No . . .
Alfred You?
Marjorie No, thanks.
Alfred Got sixpence?
Jack No.
Marjorie Here. You seen my friend?
Alfred No.
Marjorie What you in for?
Alfred In what?
Marjorie Thinks he's at home, he does. Doesn't know his own strength,
    do you?
Alfred No.
Marjorie Took a bit of his brain, haven't they?
Alfred Yeh.
Marjorie Feel better?
Alfred Yeh.
Marjorie His mother's eighty-four.
Alfred Seventy.
Marjorie Thought you said she was eighty-four.
Alfred Seventy.
Marjorie Won't know his own name soon.
Alfred You wanna fight?
Marjorie Knock you down one hand behind my back.
Alfred Garn.
Marjorie Half kill you, I will.
Alfred Go on.
Marjorie (*standing*) Wanna try?

Alfred backs off a couple of steps down R

    (*Sitting again*) Take that chair off you, you don't look out.
Jack Slight breeze. Takes the heat off the sun.
Marjorie Wanna jump on him if he bullies you.
Jack Oh, yes.
Marjorie (*to Alfred*) What you looking at then?
Alfred Sky.
Marjorie They'll lock you up if you don't look out. How old's your father?
Alfred Twenty-two.
Marjorie Older than him, are you?
Alfred Yeh.

Marjorie Older than his dad he is. Don't know where that leaves him.

Jack Hasn't been born I shouldn't wonder.

Marjorie No! (*She laughs*) Hasn't been born, he shouldn't wonder. Painted rude letters in the road.

Alfred Didn't.

Marjorie Did.

Alfred Didn't.

Marjorie Did. Right in the town centre. Took them three weeks to scrub it off.

Alfred Two.

Marjorie Three.

Alfred Two.

Marjorie Three. Apprentice painter and decorator. Didn't know what he was going to decorate. (*To Alfred*) They'll apprentice you no more. (*To Jack*) Doesn't know his own strength, he doesn't.

Jack (*looking round*) Wonder where . . .

Marjorie Send the police out for them, they will . . .

Jack Clouds . . .

Marjorie Seen it all, I have. Rape, intercourse. Physical pleasure.

Jack I had a cousin once . . .

Marjorie Here, you got a big family, haven't you?

Jack Seven brothers and sisters. Spreads around, you know.

Marjorie Here, you was an only child last week.

Jack A niece of mine—I say niece—she was only . . .

Marjorie What you do it for?

Jack Oh, now . . .

Marjorie (*to Alfred*) Wanna watch him. Trained as a doctor he has.

Jack (*gazing round*) Wonder where . . .

Marjorie (*to Alfred*) What you paint in the road?

Alfred Nothing.

Marjorie Must have painted something. Can't paint nothing. Must have painted something or they couldn't have rubbed it off.

Alfred Paint you if you don't watch out.

Marjorie I'll knock your head off.

Alfred Won't.

Marjorie Will.

Alfred Won't.

Marjorie Will.

Alfred Won't.

Marjorie What are you doing with that chair?

Alfred Nothing. (*He spins it beneath his hand*)

Jack gets up

Marjorie Faster than a rocket he is. Wanna watch him. 'Ere where you going?

Harry and Kathleen come on up R

Jack Thought I might . . . Oh . . .

Kathleen Gawd—they're coming off. I'll have nothing left . . . Oh . . .

Harry helps Kathleen to the chair

Marjorie Here, where you been?
Kathleen There and back.
Marjorie Know where you been, my girl.
Kathleen Don't.
Harry Canteen. We've . . .
Kathleen Don't tell her. Nose ten miles long she has. Trip over it one day
   she will. (*Indicating Alfred*) What's he doing?
Marjorie Won't give up his chair, he won't.
Harry Still got three, what?
Jack Yes—what. Clouds . . . (*He moves* L)
Harry Ah. Rain.
Jack Shouldn't wonder.
Marjorie Here. Put that chair down. (*She stands*)

Alfred releases the chair quickly

  (*To Jack*) You get it.
Jack Er . . . right. (*He crosses* R *and takes the chair*)

Alfred does not move

Marjorie One each, then.
Harry Yes . . .

Marjorie sits

Marjorie Well . . . (*She indicates they should sit*)

Jack and Harry sit

Kathleen Gawd . . . (*she holds her feet*)
Marjorie Had a job once.
Kathleen Gawd.
Marjorie Packing tins of food.

Alfred has moved RC

Kathleen (*to Alfred*) What you looking at?
Alfred Nothing.
Marjorie Pull your skirt down, girl.
Kathleen Got nothing up mine ain't got up yours.
Marjorie Put them in cardboard boxes.
Jack Really? I had a . . .
Marjorie Done by machine now.
Kathleen Nothing left for you to do, my girl. That's your trouble.
Marjorie 'Tis.
Kathleen Cries everywhere, she does.
Harry Oh. One has one's . . .
Kathleen Specially at Christmas. Cries at Christmas. Boxing Day. Some-
   times to New Year.

Jack Oh, well one . . .

Kathleen (*indicating Alfred*) What's he doing, then?

Marjorie Waiting to be born, he is.

Kathleen What?

Marjorie Eight o'clock tomorrow morning. Better be there. (*To Alfred*) You better be there.

Alfred Yeh.

Marjorie Late for his own birthday, he is. (*To Alfred*) Never catch up, you won't.

Harry (*holding out his hand and inspecting it*) Thought I felt—no.

Jack Could be. (*He looks up*)

Harry Lucky so far.

Jack Oh, yes.

Harry Possibility . . .

Jack By Jove . . .

Marjorie One thing you can say about this place . . .

Kathleen Yes.

Marjorie S'not like home.

Kathleen Thank Gawd.

Marjorie (*to Alfred*) What you want?

Alfred Nothing.

Kathleen Give you nothing if you come here. What you staring at?

Alfred Nothing.

Marjorie Taken off a bit of his brain they have.

Kathleen (*to Alfred*) Where they put it then?

Marjorie Thrown it in the dustbin.

Kathleen Could have done with that. Didn't cut a bit of something else off, did they. (*She laughs*)

Marjorie You know what your trouble is, my girl.

Jack Well, time for tea, very nearly (*He stands*)

Harry What? Well, yes—shouldn't wonder.

Jack Stretch the old legs . . . (*He moves down* R, *looking off*)

Harry Oh, yes.

Marjorie Not your legs need stretching ask me.

Jack Ah, well. Trim.

Marjorie Fancies himself he does.

Kathleen Don't blame him.

Marjorie Watch yourself, my girl.

Kathleen No harm come from trying.

Marjorie Good job your feet like they are, ask me.

Kathleen Have them off in the morning. Not stand this much longer.

Marjorie Slow her down: know what they're doing.

Kathleen Know what she is?

Jack Well, I . . .

Kathleen P.O.

Jack P.O.

Kathleen Persistent Offender.

Marjorie Ain't no such thing.

Kathleen Is.
Marjorie Isn't.
Kathleen Heard it in the office. Off Doctor—what's his name.
Marjorie Never heard that doctor, I haven't. Must be a new one, must that.
    Doctor what's his name is a new one on me.
Kathleen I know what I heard.

Harry dries his eyes

Marjorie Here. What's he crying about?
Kathleen Always crying one of these two.
Marjorie Call them the water babies, you ask me.
Kathleen My dad was always crying.
Marjorie Yeh?
Kathleen Drank too much, Came out of his eyes.
Marjorie Ooh!
Kathleen Here, what's the matter with you, Harry?
Harry Oh, just a er.
Jack Could have sworn . . . (*He holds out his hand and looks up*)
Kathleen S'not rain. S'him. Splashing it all over, he is.
Jack There, now . . .
Marjorie Here. Look at him: thinks it's raining.
Kathleen (*to Jack*) Here. Your friend . . .
Jack Freshening. (*He breathes deeply: fresh air exercises*)
Marjorie I don't know. What they come out for?
Kathleen Crying all over, they are. Hold his hand in a minute.
Marjorie (*to Jack*) You going to help your friend, then, are you?
Jack Oh. Comes and goes . . .
Kathleen (*to Harry*) Wanna hold my hand?

Harry does not answer

Marjorie Not seen so many tears. Haven't.
Kathleen Not since Christmas.
Marjorie Not since Christmas, girl.
Kathleen Ooooh!
Marjorie (*to Jack*) You all right?

Jack doesn't answer: stands stiffly turned away

    Think you and I better be on our way, girl.
Kathleen Think we had.
Marjorie Try and make something. What you get for it?
Kathleen Get nothing if you don't try, girl.
Marjorie No.
Kathleen Get nothing if you do, either.
Marjorie Ooooh! (*Indicating Kathleen's shoes*) Don't slow you down, do
    they? (*She stands*)
Kathleen Get my laces back or else, girl. Oh! (*To Alfred*) What you staring
    at? (*She stands*)
Alfred Nothing.

Kathleen Be dead this time tomorrow.
Marjorie No complaints then, my girl. (*Moving up* C)
Kathleen Not too soon for me.
Marjorie Going to say good-bye to your boyfriend?
Kathleen Dunno that he wants to know. Gawd! (*Moving up* C)
Marjorie Give you a hand, girl.
Kathleen Can't move without.
Marjorie On our way.
Kathleen Better get out of here, girl. Gawd! Go mad here you don't watch
out.

> *Kathleen is led off by Marjorie up* L
>   *Alfred comes up, holds the table, waits, then lifts it. He raises it above
> his head, turns, and walks off up* L

Jack By Jove. Freshening. Surprised if it doesn't blow over by tomorrow.
(*He moves* R)
Harry Oh, yes . . . (*He stirs*)
Jack Saw Harrison yesterday.
Harry Yes?
Jack Congestion.
Harry Soot.
Jack Really?
Harry Oh, yes. (*He dries his eyes*)
Jack Shouldn't wonder if wind veers. North-west.
Harry East.
Jack Really? Higher ground, of course, one notices.
Harry Found the er. (*He gestures after Marjorie and Kathleen*)
Jack Oh, yes.
Harry Extraordinary.
Jack 'Straordinary.
Harry Get used to it after a while.
Jack Oh, yes—I have a sister-in-law, for example, who wears dark
glasses.
Harry Really?
Jack Each evening before she goes to bed.
Harry Really?
Jack Following morning: takes them off.
Harry Extraordinary.
Jack Sunshine—never wears them.
Harry Well—I—extraordinary. (*He finally wipes his eyes, then puts his
handkerchief away*)
Jack The older one grows, of course—the more one takes into account
other people's foibles.
Harry Oh, yes.
Jack If a person can't be what they are, what's the purpose of being any-
thing at all?
Harry Oh, absolutely.

Alfred returns up L. *He picks up one of the metalwork chairs: turns it one way then another, gazes at them, then slowly carries it off up* L

Jack Army, I suppose, one gets quite used to foibles.
Harry Oh, yes.
Jack Navy, too, I shouldn't wonder.
Harry Oh, yes.
Jack A relative of mine rose to lieutenant-commander in a sea-going corvette.
Harry My word.
Jack In the blood.
Harry Bound to be.
Jack Oh, yes. Without the sea: hate to think.
Harry Oh, yes.
Jack At no point is one further than seventy-five miles distant from the sea.
Harry Really.
Jack That is the nature of this little island.
Harry Extraordinary when you think.
Jack When you think what came from it.
Harry Oh, yes.
Jack Radar.
Harry Oh, yes.
Jack Jet propulsion.
Harry My word.
Jack Television.
Harry Oh . . .
Jack Steam-engine.
Harry Goodness.
Jack Empire the like of which no-one has ever seen.
Harry No. My word.
Jack Light of the world.
Harry Oh, yes.
Jack Penicillin.
Harry Penicillin.
Jack Darwin.
Harry Darwin.
Jack Newton.
Harry Newton.
Jack Milton.
Harry My word.
Jack Sir Walter Raleigh.
Harry Goodness. Sir . . .
Jack Lost his head.
Harry Oh, yes.
Jack This little island.
Harry Shan't see its like.
Jack Oh, no.
Harry The sun has set. (*He rises and moves down* L)

Jack Couple of hours . . .
Harry What? (*Looking out over the audience*)
Jack One of the strange things, of course, about this place. (*He moves up* C)
Harry Oh, yes.
Jack Is its size.
Harry Yes.
Jack Never meet the same people two days running. (*He moves down* R)
Harry No.
Jack Can't find room, of course.
Harry No.
Jack See them at the gates.
Harry Oh, my word.
Jack Of an evening, looking in. Trouble is, the money isn't there.
Harry No.
Jack Exchequer. Diverting wealth to the proper . . .
Harry Oh, yes.
Jack Witness: one metalwork table, two metalwork chairs: two thousand
  people.
Harry My word, yes.
Jack While overhead . . .
Harry Oh, yes . . .

They both gaze up

  Alfred enters up L *and picks up the remaining white chair*

Alfred You finished?
Jack What . . .?
Alfred Take them back.
Harry Oh, yes . . .
Alfred Don't take them back: get into trouble.
Jack Oh, my word.

*Alfred lifts the metal chair with one hand, holding its leg, and demonstrates
his strength. Jack and Harry watch in silence*

  *Alfred lifts the chair above his head; then, still watching them, turns and
  goes off up* L

  Shadows.
Harry Yes.
Jack Another day.
Harry Ah, yes.
Jack Brother-in-law I had was an artist.
Harry Really?
Jack Would have appreciated those flowers. Light fading—clouds.
Harry Wonderful thing.
Jack Oh, yes.
Harry I should liked to have been an artist myself. Musician.
Jack Really?

Harry Flute.
Jack Beautiful instrument.
Harry Oh, yes. Shadows.
Jack (*taking the pack of cards from his pocket*) Choose any card . . . (*He goes to Harry down* L)
Harry Any?
Jack Any one . . .
Harry (*taking a card*) Yes . . . !
Jack Eight of Diamonds.
Harry My word!
Jack Right!
Harry Absolutely.
Jack Intended to show the ladies.
Harry Another day.
Jack Oh, yes. (*He re-shuffles the cards and holds them out*)
Harry Again?
Jack Any one.
Harry Er . . .
Jack Three of spades.
Harry Two of hearts.
Jack What? (*He inspects the cards briefly, then puts them away and moves* R)
Harry Amazing thing, of course, is the er.
Jack Oh, yes.
Harry Still prevails.
Jack The sea, of course, is an extraordinary . . .
Harry Oh, yes.
Jack Cousin of mine . . .
Harry See the church.

They gaze off, over the audience

Jack Shouldn't wonder He's disappointed. (*He looks up*)
Harry Oh, yes.
Jack Heart-break.
Harry Oh, yes.
Jack Same mistake. Won't make it twice.
Harry Oh, no.
Jack Once over. Never again.

Alfred comes on up L

Alfred You finished?
Jack Well, I—er . . .
Alfred Take 'em back.
Jack Oh, well. That's very . . .

Alfred grasps the two wicker chairs, glances at Jack and Harry, picks up both the chairs; glances at Jack and Harry again, holding the chairs, then takes them off up L

What I . . . er . . . yes.

Harry has begun to weep. Jack gazes off. A moment later Jack also wipes his eyes

After a while the light slowly fades

CURTAIN

FURNITURE AND PROPERTY LIST

ACT I

Scene 1

On stage: Metalwork table
2 metalwork chairs

Off stage: Newspaper (**Harry**)

Personal: **Jack:** cane
folded plastic mac
coin
playing-cards
handkerchief
Harry: leather gloves
hat
watch
handkerchief

Scene 2

Personal: **Marjorie:** bag
umbrella
Kathleen: bag

ACT II

Off stage: Wicker chair (**Harry**)
Wicker chair (**Jack**)

LIGHTING PLOT

Property fittings required: nil

ACT I Scene 1 Morning

To open:	General effect of sunny day	
Cue 1:	At end of scene	(Page 17)
	Fade to half-light, then up to previous lighting	

ACT I Scene 2 Morning

No cues

ACT II   Afternoon

To open:	Darkness	
Cue 2:	As Curtain rises	(Page 27)
	Bring up lighting to afternoon effect	
Cue 3:	**Harry:** "Canteen. We've . . ."	(Page 39)
	Dim lighting slightly	
Cue 4:	**Kathleen** and **Marjorie** exit	(Page 42)
	Start slow fade to about ½	
Cue 5:	**Jack** wipes his eyes	(Page 46)
	After a while, slow fade to Black-out	